From Your Friends at **The MA**

Weather

Grades 1–3

INVESTIGATING SCIENCE

Project Managers:
Irving P. Crump, Thad H. McLaurin

Writers:
Jennifer Overend Prior, Valerie Smith, Laura Wagner

Editors:
Cindy K. Daoust, Amy Erickson, Deborah T. Kalwat, Scott Lyons,
Jennifer Munnerlyn, Leanne Stratton, Hope H. Taylor

Art Coordinator:
Clevell Harris

Artists:
Theresa Lewis Goode, Nick Greenwood, Clevell Harris,
Rob Mayworth, Greg D. Rieves

Cover Artists:
Nick Greenwood and Kimberly Richard

www.themailbox.com

©2000 by THE EDUCATION CENTER, INC.
All rights reserved.
ISBN10 #1-56234-399-8 • ISBN13 #978-156234-399-6

Manufactured in the United States

10 9 8 7 6 5 4

Table of Contents

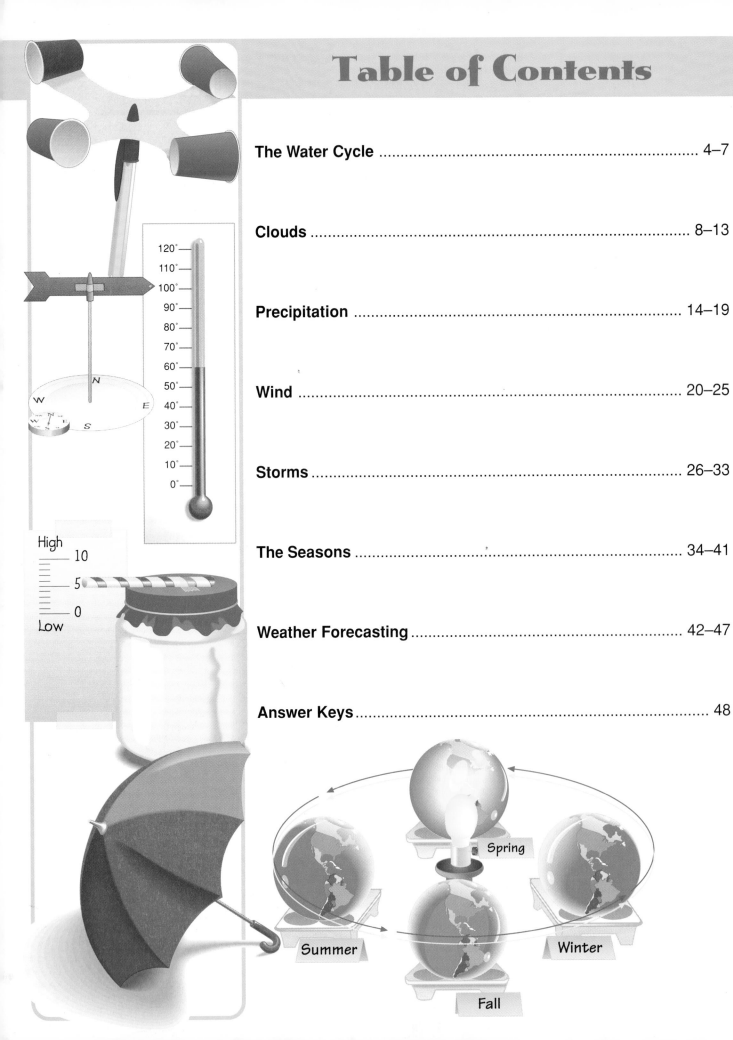

About This Book

Welcome to *Investigating Science—Weather*! This book is one of ten must-have resource books that support the National Science Education Standards and are designed to supplement and enhance your existing science curriculum. Packed with practical cross-curricular ideas and thought-provoking reproducibles, these all-new, content-specific resource books provide primary teachers with a collection of innovative and fun activities for teaching thematic science units.

Included in this book:

Investigating Science—Weather contains seven cross-curricular thematic units each containing
- Background information for the teacher
- Easy-to-implement instructions for science experiments and projects
- Student-centered activities and reproducibles
- Literature links

Cross-curricular thematic units found in this book:
- *The Water Cycle*
- *Clouds*
- *Precipitation*
- *Wind*
- *Storms*
- *The Seasons*
- *Weather Forecasting*

Other books in the primary Investigating Science series:
- *Investigating Science—Amphibians & Reptiles*
- *Investigating Science—Environment*
- *Investigating Science—Solar System*
- *Investigating Science—Insects*
- *Investigating Science—Energy, Light, & Sound*
- *Investigating Science—Plants*
- *Investigating Science—Mammals*
- *Investigating Science—Rocks & Minerals*
- *Investigating Science—Health & Safety*

The Water Cycle

Help your students learn about the water cycle one step at a time with these activities.

Background for the Teacher

- Water on the earth moves in a never-ending *cycle* (a process that happens over and over) from the sea, to the sky, to the land, and back to the sea again.
- The main processes involved in the water cycle are *precipitation, runoff, evaporation,* and *condensation.*
- Water travels to the earth in the form of *precipitation.* Rain and snow are examples of precipitation.
- Water that runs off the land into rivers or oceans is called *runoff.*
- Water at the surface of the earth turns into a gas called *water vapor* and floats back up to the sky. This process is *evaporation.*
- Water vapor *condenses,* or gathers together, into water droplets and forms clouds. Condensation is the opposite of evaporation.
- When enough water condenses in the clouds, it drops to the earth as rain.

From Books to Brains

A Drop Around the World by Barbara Shaw McKinney (Dawn Publications, 1998)

Earth: The Incredible Recycling Machine by Paul Bennett (Thomson Learning, 1993)

The Magic School Bus® Wet All Over: A Book About the Water Cycle by Joanna Cole (Scholastic Inc., 1996)

Round the Garden by Omri Glaser (Harry N. Abrams, Inc.; 1999)

Small Cloud by Ariane (Walker Publishing Company, Inc.; 1996)

Water Dance by Thomas Locker (Harcourt Brace & Company, 1997)

Watching the Water Cycle
(Experiment)

Want your students to watch the water cycle? They'll be able to when they make these terrariums. Pair students and give each pair the needed materials. Have students follow each step to create their terrariums. Instruct each pair to observe its terrarium daily for two weeks and record the findings. *(When the terrariums are put in a sunny location, the heat of the sun causes the moisture to evaporate. Water will condense on the plastic wrap and the sides of the bottle. If desired, students can gently tap the plastic wrap or bottle sides so the water drops come together, gain enough weight, and drip back into the soil. This will show the beginning of a new water cycle. The green bean seeds should begin to sprout within a week.)*

Materials for each pair:
- 1 clear plastic one-liter bottle with the top cut off
- 1 c. gravel
- 1 c. potting soil
- 2 green bean seeds
- 1/2 tsp. blood meal (a fertilizer available in most hardware or garden stores)
- 1/4 c. water
- plastic wrap
- rubber band

Steps:
1. Put the gravel in the bottle.
2. Put the soil on top of the gravel.
3. Plant the seeds with some space between them (about one-quarter inch deep).
4. Sprinkle one-half teaspoon blood meal over the soil.
5. Pour one-fourth cup water over the soil.
6. Cover the bottle with plastic wrap.
7. Secure the plastic wrap with a rubber band.
8. Put the terrarium in a sunny spot.

Wonderful Puddle Project
(Evaporation Experiment, Art)

Understanding evaporation is only one result of this experiment; cool artwork is the other. Mix food coloring and water to make three different colors (make the colors darker than you think they need to be). Pour the colored water into ice cube trays and freeze overnight. Prepare enough ice cubes so that each child will have one of each color.

On a warm sunny day, provide each child with a sheet of white construction paper. Have each student sign her paper. Then take students outside to a flat surface, such as a blacktop, and have each student secure her paper to the surface with tape. Give each child one ice cube of each color. Have the child place her ice cubes on her paper. Ask the children to predict what will happen. Ask them if they think the food coloring will evaporate with the water. Then wait one full day for the water to evaporate. Discuss with students why the water evaporated without the food coloring. *(Only pure water evaporates, filtering out such things as dirt, pollution, salt, or food coloring.)*

Jane

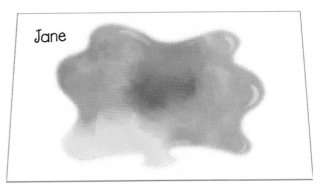

Jane

Come Together
(Condensation Demonstration)

Bring your students together to show them how water condenses. Fill two glasses halfway with warm water. Then fill one of the glasses with ice. Place both glasses in a sunny spot on a warm day and have the children observe the changes on the outside of the glasses. (Good results can be seen in about ten minutes.) Ask students how they think water gets on the outside of the glass with the ice in it but not on the glass without ice. If they think the water is seeping through the glass, pour the warm water into a new glass and the ice water into the glass that the warm water was in. Lead your students in a discussion about condensation as they watch moisture form again only on the glass with ice water. *(Explain to your students that the ice water makes the glass cold. As water vapor runs into the cold glass, the moisture in the air cools and condenses on the glass. Water molecules, bits of water too tiny to be seen, come together as they cool and form water drops.)*

Runoff Rap
(Rhyming Words)

Have your students create their very own raps about the part of the water cycle called *runoff*. Explain that some water runs off the surface of the land into streams and rivers and eventually into the oceans. Then tell students that many times this runoff carries minerals or pollution with it into the ocean. Brainstorm with the class a list of words related to runoff and words that rhyme with those words. Then divide students into groups of five. Instruct each group to come up with a rap song about water runoff using the class-created lists. After the students have finished, have each group perform its rap for the class.

Rappin' 'bout Runoff
We're gonna rap about runoff:
That's water that finds a water trough
And follows it down to the sea...
See.
It carries salt—
That's not a fault.
It's not somethin' we wanna halt.
But there's this thing called pollution,
That problem needs a solution.
Yeah, boy.
We need to try to make it right.
We can't give up; we gotta fight.
Word up.
We're gonna rap about runoff.
We're gonna rap about runoff.

An Itsy-Bitsy Water Cycle
(Review, Desktop Dramatization)

A tricycle, a bicycle, a motorcycle, an...itsy-bitsy water cycle? Explain to students that the water cycle gets its name for the circle that water travels in, just as the other "cycles" get their names from their wheels. Show students the circle made by the water cycle by making an enlarged copy of the pattern on page 7. Using the enlarged copy, create a bulletin board and ask students to help you label each of the four main steps of the water cycle. If desired, post students' dried evaporation patterns from "Wonderful Puddle Project" (page 5) around the water cycle. Then, while your students are at their desks, sing with them "The Itsy-Bitsy Spider"

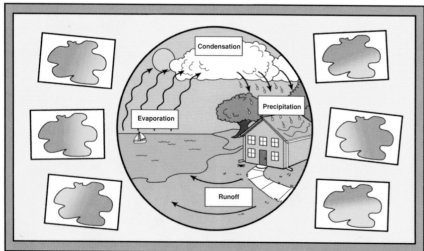

using the hand motions. Ask them to point out the different water cycle processes mentioned in the song. (Give students a hint: the song has three of the four processes.) Have students identify the processes and name them using the water cycle vocabulary they've learned (*precipitation, runoff, evaporation,* and *condensation*). Then have students identify which process is missing from "The Itsy-Bitsy Spider." *(The water cycle processes that are mentioned are* precipitation *["down came the rain"],* runoff *["and washed the spider out"], and* evaporation *["out came the sun and dried up all the rain"]. Condensation is missing from the rhyme.)*

Pattern

Use with "An Itsy-Bitsy Water Cycle" on page 6.
Or duplicate for each child to complete and color independently.

| Precipitation | Condensation | Evaporation | Runoff |

Clouds

Use this collection of fun, foamy, frosty activities to introduce students to the wonderful world of clouds.

 ## Background for the Teacher

- *Clouds* are clusters of tiny water droplets in the air.
- Clouds form as water vapor rises and condenses into liquid.
- There are three main groups of clouds: *stratus, cumulus,* and *cirrus.* They are categorized by their shape, altitude, and potential to produce rain or snow.
- *Meteorologists* use clouds in making weather predictions.
- Clouds act like a blanket for the earth, keeping the sun's heat out during the day and keeping warm air close to the ground at night.
- *Fog* is a cloud near the earth's surface.

Clouds of Foam
(Literature, Writing, Art)

Your students will love listening to a good story and creating foamy clouds on their desks! Introduce students to clouds and build writing skills with this creative hands-on activity. You will need two cans of nonmenthol shaving cream, paper towels, and a paper cloud cutout for each student. Begin by reading *The Cloud Book* by Tomie dePaola. After reading and discussing the book, squirt a puff of shaving cream on each student's desk. Then, as you reread the description of each cloud type, have your youngsters create the clouds with shaving cream. As students wipe off their desks with the paper towels, distribute the paper cloud cutouts. Instruct each student to write a newly learned cloud fact on her cutout. When the clouds are complete, invite each student to share her fact with the class. Then have each child tape her cloud fact on a classroom window.

 ## Cloud Book Nook

The Cloud Book by Tomie dePaola (Holiday House, Inc.; 1985)

Fog, Mist and Smog (Living With the Weather Series) by Andrew Dunn (Raintree Steck-Vaughn Publishers, 1998)

Little Cloud by Eric Carle (Philomel Books, 1996)

Sector 7 by David Wiesner (Clarion Books, 1999)

Wind and Rain (Why Do We Have? Series) by Claire Llewellyn (Barron's Educational Series, Inc.; 1995)

I Know What Cloud That Must Be
(sung to the tune of "My Bonnie Lies Over the Ocean")

Verse:
I see clouds in the sky stretched like blankets.
I see clouds in the sky looking gray.
I see clouds in the sky bringing raindrops.
Those must be [stratus] clouds I see.

Chorus:
Must be, must be,
Those must be [stratus] clouds I see, I see.
Must be, must be,
Those must be [stratus] clouds I see.

Verse:
I see clouds in the sky that look puffy.
I see clouds in the sky that are fat.
I see clouds that look just like cotton.
Those must be [cumulus] clouds I see.

Chorus: [cumulus]

Verse:
I see clouds in the sky that look wispy.
I see clouds in the sky that look thin.
I see clouds that look just like feathers.
Those must be [cirrus] clouds I see.

Chorus: [cirrus]

Sing a Song of Cloud Types
(Reading, Singing)

Puffy, fluffy, feathery, bumpy…there are so many different kinds of clouds! Singing this simple song is just the key to teaching the three main groups of clouds to your students. Ahead of time, copy the lyrics on a chart and create simple drawings of the three cloud types as shown. Remind students that the three main families of clouds are *stratus*, *cumulus*, and *cirrus*. Review each cloud family's characteristics: stratus clouds form in low, gray blankets; cumulus clouds are white and puffy; and cirrus clouds are thin and feathery. Then have students sing the song, each time substituting different cloud words in the chorus.

Cooking Up a Cloud
(Demonstration)

Ask your students these questions: Have you ever noticed fog on a bathroom mirror? Did you ever create a cloud with your breath on a cold day? Did you ever watch the steam rise as you waited for a cup of hot chocolate to cool? Explain to students that as warm air rises, it carries water vapor. As the water vapor rises, it cools and changes back to water droplets which gather together to form clouds. Follow the steps below to demonstrate one way clouds form.

Materials: one 12" x 18" sheet of dark-colored construction paper, 1 clear jar, pitcher of hot water, 12 ice cubes, 1 pie tin

Directions:
1. Pour the hot water into the jar until it is three-fourths full.
2. Put the jar in front of the construction paper to make the cloud easier for students to see.
3. Put the ice in the pie tin and place it on top of the jar of hot water.
4. Watch as a cloud quickly appears! *(As the warm, moist air in the jar meets the cold air at the top, it cools. It is unable to hold all its water vapor so some of it condenses.)*

Clouds Up Close
(Experiments)

Circulate small groups of students through centers featuring experiments that introduce them to cloud formation. Ahead of time, gather the materials listed for each activity and place each set in a center. Begin by explaining that clouds, fog, and mist are made up of tiny water droplets. These water droplets form when warm, moist air, called water vapor, meets cooler air. The cooling water vapor *condenses* (changes from gas to liquid) into water droplets or ice crystals.

Divide students into four groups and assign a starting center for each group. Explain the directions for each center's experiment. After completing an experiment, have each child create a diagram showing the cool surface; the warm, moist air; and the surface on which the water vapor collects. (While the students record their observations, dry the eyeglasses in center 3 and the glasses in center 4.)

Center 1 (Adult Supervision Required)
Materials: 1 large, clear, glass jar with a straw-sized hole in the lid; straw; candle; matches; oven mitts

With the children at a safe distance, light the candle. Using oven mitts, hold the jar's mouth over the flame for about 20 seconds. Blow out the candle. Put the lid on the jar and cover its hole. Let the jar cool for about a minute. Insert the straw through the hole and exhale several times into the jar. Set the jar on a flat surface and have students observe it. *(The air in the jar contains particles of soot from the candle. A cloud forms when the warm, moist air in the jar cools suddenly and condenses onto the soot particles. Condensation appears on the surface of the glass.)*

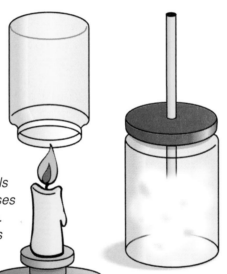

Center 2
Materials: 2 empty smooth-sided cans, ice cubes, paper towels

Have students take turns warming one can by rolling it between their hands for two minutes. Meanwhile, chill the other can by filling it with ice cubes. Remove the ice cubes from the can. Have one student exhale on the cold can and show the resulting moisture to the group. Then have another student exhale on the warm can and show the results. *(The warm, moist exhaled air contains water vapor that condenses onto the cold can's cooler surface, leaving tiny droplets of water. The water vapor from exhaled air on the warm can evaporates quickly or doesn't condense at all. This is why there is more moisture on the cold can.)*

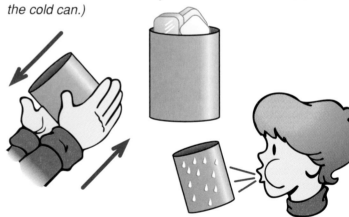

Center 3
Materials: eyeglasses, ice cubes in a covered pan

Have one group member carefully place the eyeglasses facedown on the ice in the pan and then re-cover the pan. After waiting two minutes, have another child remove the eyeglasses and allow the other group members to observe the lenses. *(Fog appears on the eyeglass lenses because the warmer air in the room condenses onto the colder surface of the glass lenses.)*

Center 4
Materials: 2 clear drinking glasses, warm water, ice water

Half-fill one glass with warm water and the other with ice water. Have students watch the glasses for three minutes. Then have each child in the group touch the outside of each glass. *(The water vapor in the air touches the cold water glass and is cooled. It condenses making the outside of the glass wet. Droplets don't form on the warm water glass because the air around it is not cooled.)*

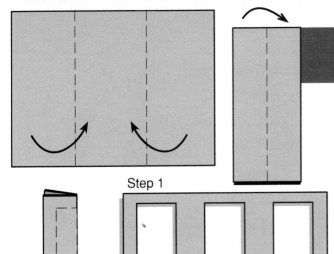

Cloudy Weather Windows
(Critical Thinking, Art)

Step 1

Step 2

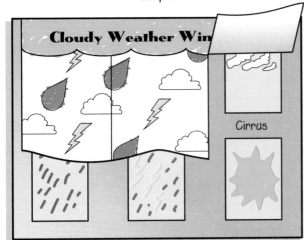

Use this attractive art project to help your students associate cloud types with the weather they bring. Begin by reviewing these three cloud types: *stratus*, *cumulonimbus*, and *cirrus*. Then guide students through the steps below to create cloudy weather windows. Display the projects in your classroom before allowing each child to take his project home to share with his family.

Materials for each student: 1 copy of page 13, 1 brown and 1 light blue 9" x 11" sheet of construction paper, 1 sticky note smudged with artist's charcoal, fist-sized ball of cotton batting, scissors, glue, crayons or markers

1. Fold the brown paper in thirds. Then fold it in half as shown.
2. At the fold, draw two rectangles. Cut out the rectangles and unfold the paper to reveal six windows as shown.
3. Glue the brown paper to the blue paper.
4. Shape a stratus cloud from batting. Rub it on the charcoal and glue it in the first window. Draw tiny drops of rain in the window under the stratus cloud. Label the cloud.
5. Shape a puffy cumulonimbus cloud and rub it on the charcoal. Glue it in the second window. Draw lightning and rain in the window under the cumulonimbus cloud. Add a label.
6. In the third window, glue wisps of batting to represent cirrus clouds. In the window under the cirrus clouds, draw the sun. Add a label.
7. Color and cut out the curtains. Then cut between the curtains on the dotted lines. Glue the top edge of the curtains along the top edge of the windows.

Cozy Cloud Blankets
(Demonstration)

Are cloudy or clear nights on earth cooler? Use this simple demonstration to show your students that clouds form a natural blanket around the earth. Follow up the demonstration with a discussion, guiding students to conclude that clear nights are cooler because there is no blanket of clouds to hold the heat near the earth's surface. Then have each child create an illustration, demonstrating his understanding that this cozy blanket of clouds helps keep the earth warm.

Materials: two 16-oz. glass jars, hot water, 2 thermometers, large handful of cotton batting, watch

Steps:
1. Half-fill each jar with hot water. (Warn students not to touch the jars.)
2. Place a thermometer in each jar. After several minutes, have a student volunteer record each thermometer's temperature on a chart. Then cover one jar with the batting.
3. Check and record each jar's temperature at 5-, 10-, and 15-minute intervals.
4. Compare and discuss the results. Guide students to conclude that the batting, like clouds over the earth's surface, helps to keep heat in the jar.

Cloud Journal

You can read signs in the clouds to predict weather just like a meteorologist! Keep a cloud journal for five days. Each day, draw the clouds and use the Cloud Clues below to help you name them. Then guess what weather might be coming your way. An example has been done for you.

Cloud Clues

stratus	cumulus	cirrus
gray and gloomy	fair weather	fair weather
nimbostratus	cumulonimbus	cirrostratus
fog, rain, or snow	rain, thunder, and lightning	soon it will rain

Today is __Friday__.
I see __cumulus__ clouds.

I think tomorrow will be __fair__.

Today is _____.
I see _____ clouds.

I think tomorrow will be _____.

Today is _____.
I see _____ clouds.

I think tomorrow will be _____.

Today is _____.
I see _____ clouds.

I think tomorrow will be _____.

Today is _____.
I see _____ clouds.

I think tomorrow will be _____.

Today is _____.
I see _____ clouds.

I think tomorrow will be _____.

Cloudy Weather Windows

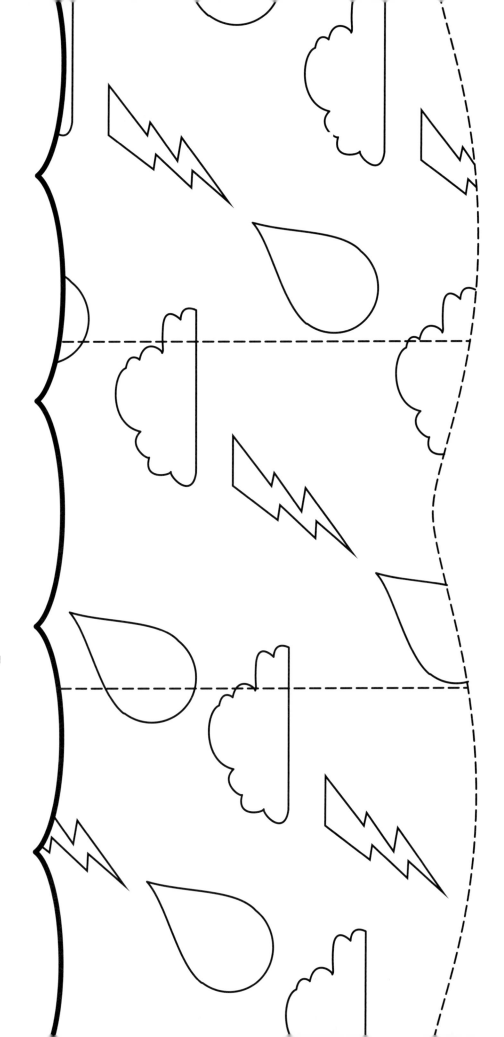

Note to the teacher: Use with "Cloudy Weather Windows" on page 11.

Precipitation

Pitter-patter! Splish, splash! A downpour of learning fun is headed your way with these precipitation ideas and reproducibles!

Background for the Teacher

- *Precipitation* is water that falls from clouds. The temperature determines whether it falls as rain, snow, sleet, or hail.
- *Rain,* the most common type of precipitation, forms when water droplets combine or when ice melts.
- A *snowflake* is formed when tiny ice crystals freeze together. About one-fifth of the earth's surface is covered by snow.
- The record for the greatest snowfall in a 24-hour period was set in 1921 when 76 inches fell in Colorado.
- *Sleet* is formed when rain freezes or when partially melted snowflakes refreeze. It usually falls during the winter.
- Rounded pieces of ice that are formed by updrafts in thunderstorms are called *hailstones.* Hail is most common in the summer.
- The largest hailstone on record weighed about 1½ pounds and was bigger than a softball. Hailstones can fall at more than 100 mph, causing injuries and damaging crops or property.
- In 1882 some very unusual hailstones fell in Iowa. Small frogs were found inside them!

Oh, the Weather Outside...
(Recognizing the Effects of Precipitation)

What difference does precipitation make? Plenty! Use this cause-and-effect activity to explore the influence precipitation (or the lack of it) has on people, plants, and animals. Share the background information on this page. As students brainstorm effects of precipitation, list them on the board. Point out that some effects are positive while others are negative.

To further explore the far-reaching effects of precipitation, divide students into small groups. Assign each group a condition such as heavy rain or no rain for months. The students in each group label a large sheet of paper with the condition. They list possible effects of the condition and then add an illustration. After each group shares its work with the class, display the posters below the title "What a Difference Precipitation Makes!"

Precipitation...

- helps crops grow
- can cause cancellations
- provides drinking water
- can cause floods
- makes the grass green
- h

A Literary Cloudburst

Come On, Rain! by Karen Hesse (Scholastic Inc., 1999)
Down Comes the Rain (Let's-Read-and-Find-Out Science® series) by Franklyn M. Branley (HarperCollins Publishers, Inc.; 1997)
Listen to the Rain by Bill Martin Jr. and John Archambault (Henry Holt and Company, 1988)
Snow and Ice (Living With the Weather series) by Philip Steele (Raintree Steck-Vaughn Publishers, 1998)
Snowflake Bentley by Jacqueline Briggs Martin (Houghton Mifflin Company, 1998)

Window on the Weather
(Observing and Recording Precipitation, Using Precise Words)

Sharpen your young meteorologists' observation skills with precipitation logs! Display a jumbo umbrella cutout labeled "Precipitation." Tell students that there are four basic types of precipitation: rain, snow, sleet, and hail. Ask students to brainstorm words that describe various types of precipitation. Record them on the cutout. Then have each student use the materials and follow the directions shown to make a precipitation log.

On each of the next five school days that precipitation occurs, the youngster writes the date on a page in his log. He describes the precipitation, referring to the brainstormed list as necessary for precise words, then illustrates his work. Not only will students become better weather watchers, they'll boost their descriptive-writing skills, too!

Materials for each student:
two 9" x 12" sheets of brown construction paper
two ³/₄" x 12" brown construction paper strips
six 8¹/₂" x 11" sheets of white paper
two 4¹/₂" x 9" pieces of colored construction paper
crayons
glue
access to a stapler
scissors

Directions:
1. On a sheet of white paper, illustrate a scene that shows one type of precipitation.
2. Glue the illustration onto a sheet of brown paper.
3. Glue on brown paper strips so the picture resembles a window frame.
4. Cut the colored paper to make two curtains. Glue the curtains onto the window as shown.
5. Stack five sheets of white paper on the second sheet of brown paper. Place the window on top. Staple the entire stack along the top edge.

Looks Like Rain!
(Observing, Drawing Conclusions)

All clouds have water, so why doesn't it rain more often? Find out with this demonstration! After posing the question to students, invite them to share their ideas. Then pair youngsters and give each twosome a plastic lid, an eyedropper, a small container of water, and a paper towel to place on the work surface. One student in each twosome uses the eyedropper to make water droplets of assorted sizes on the lid. As her partner watches closely, the youngster quickly turns the lid over and holds it above the paper towel. The students observe what happens, dry the lid, trade roles, and repeat the process.

Invite students to share their observations. Lead them to conclude that only the large drops fell. Explain that, similarly, only the heavy droplets in a cloud fall. Tiny droplets need to combine with other droplets to increase their weight before they are able to fall as rain. It takes more than a million cloud droplets to make one raindrop. Now that's a watery wonder!

Going Down!
(Making Predictions, Demonstration)

The race is on! Which will fall faster: a snowflake or a raindrop? Ask each student to use a snowflake or raindrop cutout to record his prediction on a class graph. To check the predictions, give each student a piece of white paper to represent a snowflake and an equal-sized piece of blue paper to represent a raindrop. The youngster crumples the blue paper into a ball. Then he holds the paper ball and white paper at the same level above his head. At a predetermined signal, the student drops the papers and observes which one reaches the floor first. Ask students to share their results and compare them with the predictions. Then explain that the snowflake has a larger surface than the raindrop. It moves more slowly because it has more air resistance. What a winning way to investigate precipitation rates!

Frosty Figures
(Identifying Types of Snowflakes, Comprehension)

From long and pointy to short and capped, snowflakes come in countless shapes and sizes. In fact, no two are exactly alike! Explore some of the basic snowflake shapes with this sparkling booklet project. To begin, tell students that all snowflakes have six sides, but every snowflake is unique. A snowflake's shape is determined by where the snowflake is formed and the temperature of the clouds it travels through as it falls. Post a chart like the one shown and review the information with students. Point out that there are variations of the basic shapes because snowflakes change shape as they fall. Then have each student use the materials and directions shown to make a snowflake-filled booklet.

Materials for each student:
one 6" x 18" piece of blue construction paper
1 copy of page 18
silver or white glitter
white paint
cotton swabs and empty plastic thread spools
glue
scissors

Directions:
1. Use the Word Bank to complete each sentence on page 18.
2. Cut along the bold lines.
3. Accordion-fold the blue paper into four equal-sized sections as shown.
4. Sign the title box and then glue it onto the cover. Unfold the paper.
5. Glue a snowflake picture on each section and glue the matching set of sentences below it.
6. Turn the strip facedown. Use cotton swabs, spools, and paint to decorate the paper with snowflakes.
7. Sprinkle glitter onto the wet paint. Carefully shake off any extra glitter.
8. After the paint is dry, refold the booklet.

Snowflakes		
Where Formed	**Shape**	**Illustration**
high clouds	capped columns	
middle clouds	hexagonal plates	
low clouds	starlike crystals, needles, hexagonal plates	

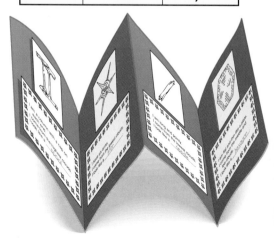

What a Ride!
(Making and Explaining a Model)

Hailstones are created in what could be called nature's wildest rides—thunderstorms! Invite students to track the rides of model hailstones with this partner activity. Tell students that a hailstone is formed during a thunderstorm when ice freezes around a particle such as dust. Gusts of wind cause the hailstone to move up into cold air and down into warmer air a number of times. Each time it rises or falls, another layer of ice forms around it. Milky layers form at high altitudes and clear layers form at low altitudes.

To make a clay hailstone, give each pair of students approximately two ounces each of white and colored clay to represent high- and low-altitude ice, respectively. One student in each twosome makes a small ball of white clay. Her partner forms a layer of colored clay around it. The partners continue alternating layers until they have used all of their clay. Then one partner carefully uses a plastic knife to cut the resulting clay hailstone in half. To summarize its hailstone's travels, each twosome cuts a cloud from gray construction paper. The youngsters make a dot either high or low on the cloud to represent each trip the hailstone made. They connect the dots as shown. Display each twosome's hailstone with its cloud; then invite students to compare the hailstones' stormy travels.

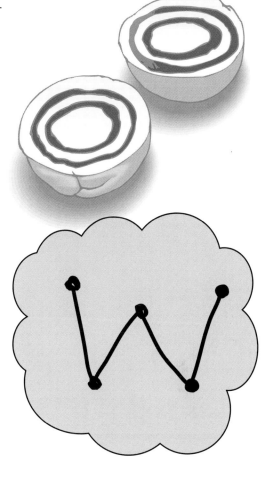

Weather Word Wheel
(Identifying Precipitation Terms)

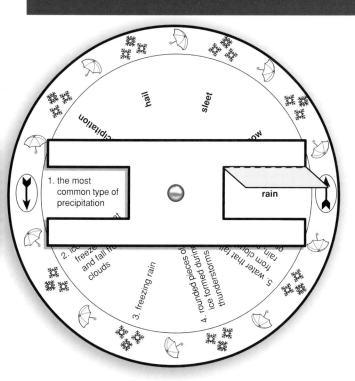

What's in the forecast? A self-checking precipitation review! Give each student a copy of page 19. The youngster colors the patterns, being careful to leave the words visible. He cuts along the bold lines and then folds the window flap up at the dashed line. He uses a brad to attach the window strip atop the wheel. The youngster turns the wheel in the direction indicated until the first definition is revealed in the window without a flap. He silently reads the definition, guesses the corresponding word, and then lifts the flap to check his answer. The student continues with the remaining definitions and words in a like manner.

For additional practice, pair students. One student in each pair rolls a die. He turns the wheel so that the definition with the same number is shown in the window that does not have a flap. (If he rolls a six, he turns the wheel to a definition of his choice.) The student reads the definition to his partner. After the partner guesses the word, the first student lifts the flap to check the answer. Partners switch roles and take turns in a like manner for a desired period of time.

Booklet Patterns

Use with "Frosty Figures" on page 16.

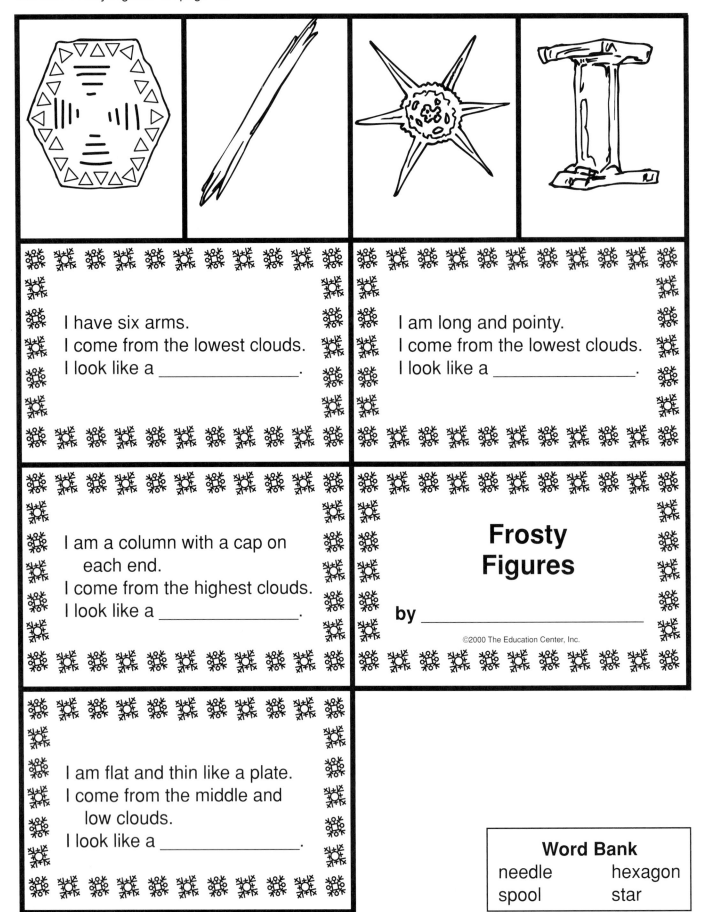

I have six arms.
I come from the lowest clouds.
I look like a _____.

I am long and pointy.
I come from the lowest clouds.
I look like a _____.

I am a column with a cap on
   each end.
I come from the highest clouds.
I look like a _____.

**Frosty
Figures**

by _____

I am flat and thin like a plate.
I come from the middle and
   low clouds.
I look like a _____.

Word Bank	
needle	hexagon
spool	star

Wheel

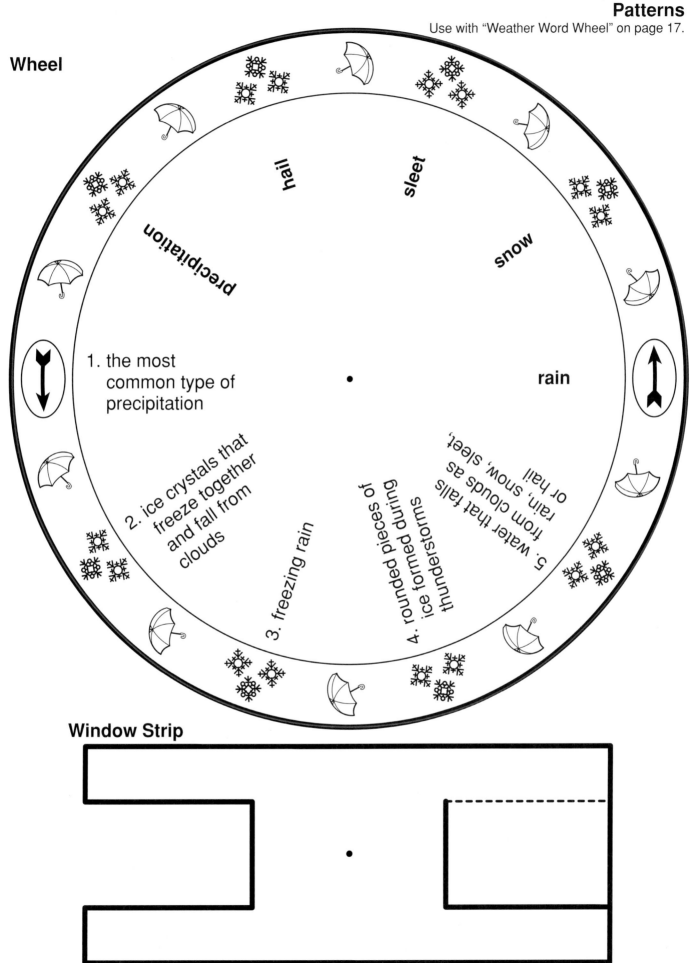

hail

sleet

precipitation

snow

1. the most common type of precipitation

rain

2. ice crystals that freeze together and fall from clouds

3. freezing rain

4. rounded pieces of ice formed during thunderstorms

5. water that falls from clouds as rain, snow, sleet, or hail

Window Strip

Wind

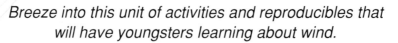

Breeze into this unit of activities and reproducibles that will have youngsters learning about wind.

Background for the Teacher

- *Wind* is moving air.
- Wind is caused by uneven heating of the air around the earth by the sun. As warm air expands and rises, an area of *low pressure* is created. Cooler, heavier air rushes into the areas of low pressure, producing wind.
- *Wind direction* is the direction *from* which the wind is blowing. A *weather vane* detects wind direction.
- *Circulation* occurs when warm air rises and cool air flows in to replace it. Circulation over the entire earth is called *general circulation*.
- *Wind speed* is the rate of the air's motion. An *anemometer* measures wind speed.
- The *Beaufort wind scale* is a series of names and numbers that indicate wind speeds based on the observable effects of the wind.

Creating Artificial Wind
(Demonstration)

Use this simple demonstration to show students how wind is created. Explain that wind is produced when an area of cooler, heavier air rushes into an area of warmer low-pressure air. For example, the breeze felt at the beach is produced when the sun's rays warm the air above land more than the air above the water. The warmer air above the land expands and rises, creating a low-pressure area. The cooler air above the water moves into the low-pressure area over the land, creating wind.

Provide each student with a balloon. Have each student blow up her balloon and pinch the opening to keep the air inside. Instruct the child to feel the side of the balloon. Have her determine whether the high-pressure air is inside or outside the balloon. *(The high-pressure air is inside the balloon.)* Direct the child to place her hand near the opening of the balloon and then release the air inside. Have the student explain how the "wind" was created. *(The high-pressure air inside the balloon rushed into the low-pressure area outside of the balloon.)*

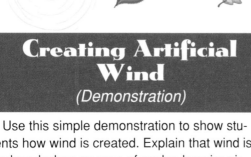

Breezy Books

Can You See the Wind? (Rookie Read-About Science® series) by Allan Fowler (Children's Press, 1999)

Feel the Wind (Let's-Read-and-Find-Out Science® series) by Arthur Dorros (HarperTrophy, 1990)

The Gates of the Wind by Kathryn Lasky (Harcourt Brace & Company, 1995)

Millicent and the Wind by Robert Munsch (Annick Press Ltd., 1984)

The Usborne Book of Kites by Susan Mayes (Usborne Publishing Limited, 1992)

The Whirlys and the West Wind by Christine Ross (Houghton Mifflin Company, 1993)

Weather Vane
(Making an Instrument, Experiment)

Learning wind direction is a breeze with these student-made weather vanes. Explain to students that the direction a weather vane points is the direction *from* which the wind is blowing. Then divide students into small groups. Distribute the materials listed to each group; then have students follow the steps below for making and using a weather vane. Record student findings on a class chart.

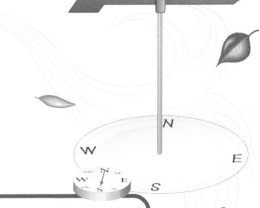

Materials for each group:
length of cardboard
pen cap
chopstick
small ball of clay
paper plate
pencil
compass
scissors
tape

Steps:
1. Cut an arrow from the cardboard; then press the ball of clay on the arrow tip. Tape the pen cap to the middle of the arrow.
2. Label the paper plate around the rim with the cardinal directions as shown.
3. Place the pen cap and arrow on top of the chopstick.
4. Take the weather vane, paper plate, pencil, and compass outdoors to an open area.
5. Using the compass, position the paper plate on the ground so the cardinal directions on the plate match the directions on the compass.
6. Poke a hole in the center of the plate with a pencil. Then push the chopstick through the hole and into the ground.
7. Use the weather vane to gather wind direction data.

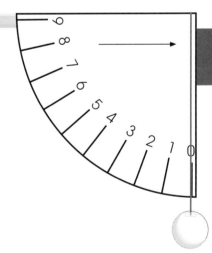

Measuring Wind Speed
(Making an Instrument, Experiment)

Help your students gauge wind speed by making anemometers. Explain that an *anemometer* is an instrument that scientists use to measure how fast air moves. To make an anemometer, each pair of students will need a tagboard copy of page 24, one $7\frac{1}{2}$-inch length of thread, one $1\frac{1}{2}$-inch Styrofoam® ball, an unsharpened pencil, scissors, and tape. Direct students to cut out the pattern and recording strip along the bold lines. Have each pair tape the anemometer pattern to the pencil as shown. Then have the pair tape one end of the thread to the Styrofoam ball and the opposite end to the corner of the pattern, making sure the thread falls across the zero mark.

Next, take your youngsters outside. Instruct one student from each pair to face the wind while he points the arrow on the anemometer in the direction from which the wind blows. Have the other student observe the string as the wind blows the ball. Instruct the observer to notice where the string crosses the scale. Then direct students to record their findings in the appropriate box on the recording strip. After one week of testing, discuss the results to determine which days were breeziest and which days were more calm.

Windy Matchup
(Game)

Put the pieces together for lots of learning with this Beaufort wind scale self-checking game. In advance, make an enlarged copy of the Beaufort wind scale. Then make one tagboard copy of page 25. Cut the pieces apart along the dotted lines; then place the game pieces and the wind scale in a center. Explain to students that Sir Francis Beaufort created this scale for determining wind speed. Observable effects indicate the speed at which winds blow. Discuss the scale with students; then explain the game directions below. In turn, send student pairs to the center to play the game.

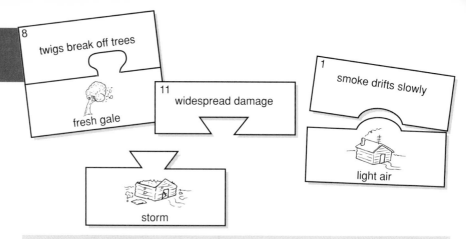

Game directions:
1. Use the Beaufort wind scale to complete each puzzle by matching the written observation with the correct picture and description. *(You've made a match if the pieces fit together like a puzzle.)*
2. Lay the completed puzzles in order from weakest winds to strongest ones.

Beaufort Wind Scale

Number	Speed/MPH	Description	Observation
0	less than 1	calm	smoke rises vertically
1	1–3	light air	smoke drifts slowly
2	4–7	light breeze	leaves rustle; wind felt on face
3	8–12	gentle breeze	leaves and small twigs move
4	13–18	moderate breeze	small branches move
5	19–24	fresh breeze	small trees sway
6	25–31	strong breeze	large branches sway
7	32–38	moderate gale	whole trees sway; difficult to walk against wind
8	39–46	fresh gale	twigs break off trees
9	47–54	strong gale	shingles blown off roof
10	55–63	whole gale	trees uprooted
11	64–73	storm	widespread damage
12–17	74 and above	hurricane	extreme damage

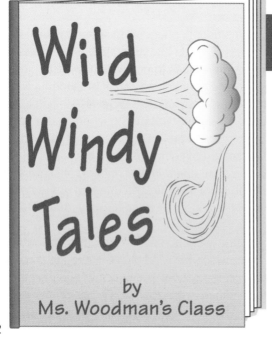

Wind Tales
(Cooperative Creative Writing)

Discover just how creative your young writers are when they participate in this cooperative-writing activity! Divide students into groups of three. Discuss the ways wind works for us, such as blowing seeds away from the parent plant, turning a windmill, pushing sailboats, and flying kites.

Have each child begin writing a story about one way wind works for us. After five minutes have each student stop writing and pass his paper to the group member on his right. Have the second student continue writing the story that was passed to him. After another five minutes, direct each student to pass his paper to the right one more time. Instruct the third student to read the wind story and then add an ending. After the third student has finished writing, instruct him to return the story to the group member who began it. Then invite all students to share their collaborative stories with the class. Bind the pages to make a class book titled "Wild Windy Tales."

Windy Writing
(Creative Writing, Art)

Enthusiasm will circulate with this creative-writing activity that has students' stories flying high on kites. In advance, gather one sheet of construction paper and a length of yarn for each child. Read to students the book *Millicent and the Wind* by Robert Munsch. Then discuss the unusual ways the wind interacted with Millicent. Have each child brainstorm ways the wind could play with her. Instruct the child to write a story about an adventurous day with the wind. Next, have her fold the construction paper lengthwise. Direct her to cut the corners opposite the fold to make a kite shape as shown. Have the student glue her story in the center of the kite. Direct her to tape the length of yarn to the bottom of the kite. Have the child cut bow shapes from construction paper scraps and then tape them to the yarn to complete the kite tail. Display the stories on a bulletin board titled "Windy Writing."

Wonderful Windsocks
(Arts and Crafts)

Your youngsters will be eager to fill the sky with these beautiful windsocks! Gather the materials listed and then guide each child through the steps below.

Materials needed for each child:
16" x 24" piece of white plastic garbage bag
1"-wide plastic ring cut from a two-liter soda bottle
two 12" lengths of string
glue stick
permanent markers
scissors
hole puncher

Steps:
1. Decorate the plastic with permanent markers; then turn it over.
2. Apply glue to the edge of one of the short sides of the bag.
3. Starting at one end of the glued edge, carefully roll the plastic ring from one end to the other.
4. Apply glue to the overlapping long edge of plastic. Carefully press the edges together to create a tube.
5. Fringe-cut the bottom of the windsock.
6. Punch two holes opposite each other on the plastic ring.
7. Tie one length of string to the ring; then tie the second length of string to the center of the first one as shown.
8. Take your windsock outdoors and run with the wind!

23

Pattern and Recording Strip

Use with "Measuring Wind Speed" on page 21.

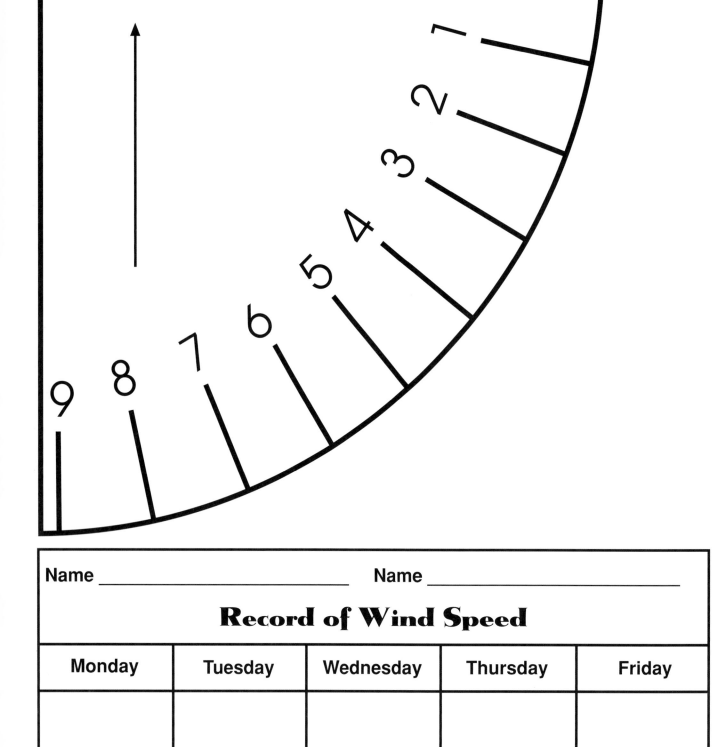

Name _____   **Name** _____

Record of Wind Speed

Monday	Tuesday	Wednesday	Thursday	Friday

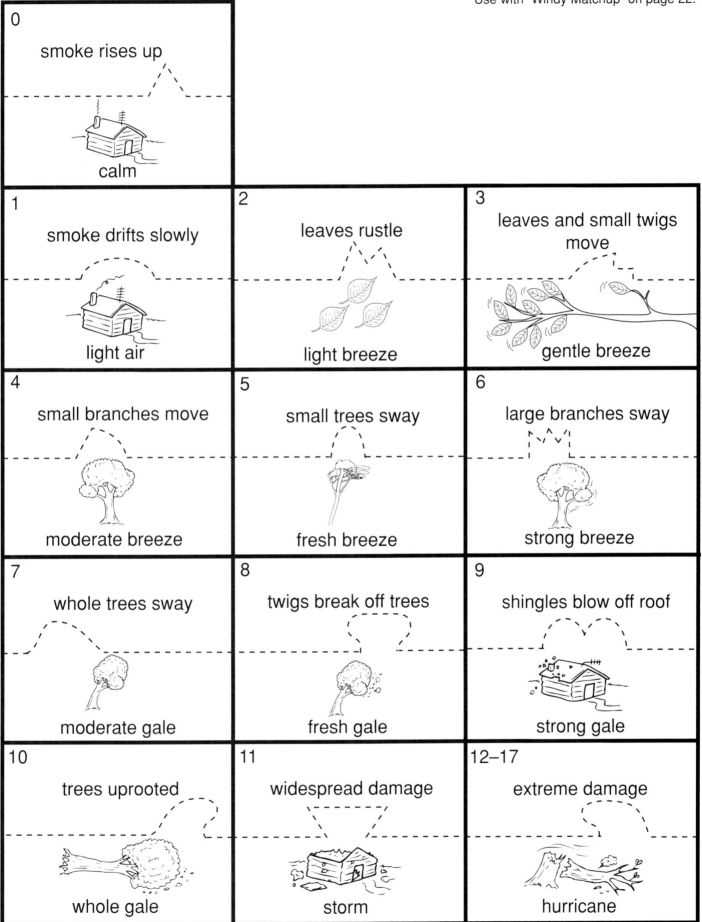

0 smoke rises up
calm

1 smoke drifts slowly
light air

2 leaves rustle
light breeze

3 leaves and small twigs move
gentle breeze

4 small branches move
moderate breeze

5 small trees sway
fresh breeze

6 large branches sway
strong breeze

7 whole trees sway
moderate gale

8 twigs break off trees
fresh gale

9 shingles blow off roof
strong gale

10 trees uprooted
whole gale

11 widespread damage
storm

12–17 extreme damage
hurricane

Storms

The forecast calls for educational fun when you use these activities, ideas, and reproducibles to teach students about storms!

It Was a Dark and Stormy Night...

(Exploring Prior Knowledge, Graphing)

Find out what your weather watchers already know about storms with this great graphing activity! Display a grid like the one shown. Lead the class in a discussion of the definition of each storm listed on the grid. Next, have each child place a personalized sticky note next to each of the storms that he has experienced. Discuss the resulting graph with the class.

Next, invite each student to pen an account of his most memorable storm experience on provided paper. Allow time for each child to share his story with the class.

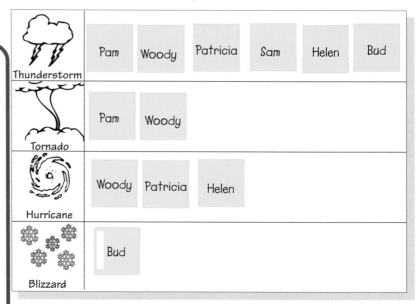

Thunderstorm	Pam	Woody	Patricia	Sam	Helen	Bud
Tornado	Pam	Woody				
Hurricane	Woody	Patricia	Helen			
Blizzard	Bud					

Background for the Teacher

- Each year, about 16 million thunderstorms occur around the world.
- Every second of every day the earth is struck by lightning an average of 100 times!
- In the United States, about 100 people are killed by lightning strikes each year.
- Tornado winds can blow up to 300 miles per hour.
- An average of 800 tornadoes occur in the United States each year.
- More tornadoes occur in the United States than in any other country.
- Tropical storms become hurricanes when their wind speeds reach 74 miles per hour.
- Names for hurricanes are assigned in alphabetical order. They alternate between a boy's name and a girl's name. Each year, the list begins again with an *a* name. There are two lists: one for hurricanes that form over the Pacific Ocean and one for hurricanes that form over the Atlantic Ocean.
- An average of four to five hurricanes form in the Atlantic Ocean each year.
- A storm is called a blizzard when there's a substantial snowfall and wind speeds of 35 miles per hour. The temperature is as low as 10°F.

Stormy Weather Reading

The Big Storm by Bruce Hiscock (Aladdin Paperbacks, 2000)

Hurricane! by Jonathan London (Lothrop, Lee & Shepard Books; 1998)

Hurricanes & Tornadoes (The Wonders of Our World series) by Neil Morris (Crabtree Publishing Company, 1998)

The Magic School Bus® Inside a Hurricane by Joanna Cole (Scholastic Inc., 1996)

The Magic School Bus® Kicks Up a Storm by Nancy White (Scholastic Inc., 2000)

Storms by Seymour Simon (Mulberry Books, 1992)

Wild Weather: Blizzards! (Hello Reader! Science series, Level 4) by Lorraine Jean Hopping (Cartwheel Books, 1999)

A Thunderstorm Is Building
(Understanding Thunderstorms)

What causes all of the crashing and flashing that happens during a thunderstorm? Give students the explanation for thunder and lightning with this breezy art activity! Begin by reading aloud *Flash, Crash, Rumble, and Roll* by Franklyn Mansfield Branley (HarperCollins Children's Books, 1999). Reinforce the information in the book by guiding students through the steps listed to create thunderstorm mobiles. Suspend the completed mobiles above the children's desks.

Materials for each student:
1 copy of page 31
six 5" x 7" gray construction paper rectangles
two 5" x 7" white construction paper rectangles
one 28" length of yarn
yellow construction paper scraps
scissors
glue

Directions:
1. Use the cloud pattern from page 31 and the construction paper rectangles to make six gray cloud shapes and two white cloud shapes.
2. Tie a small loop at one end of the length of yarn.
3. Sandwich the length of yarn between the white clouds and glue the clouds together so that they hang about one inch below the loop.
4. Sandwich the length of yarn between two of the gray clouds and glue the clouds together so that they hang about two inches below the white cloud. In the same manner, glue each of the other sets of gray clouds.
5. Cut the cards apart. Glue card number one on the white cloud. Glue each of the remaining cards in numerical order on the gray clouds.
6. Make a lightning bolt out of yellow construction paper. Glue the bolt on the second gray cloud.
7. Read the cards aloud to a partner.

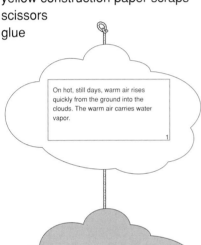

On hot, still days, warm air rises quickly from the ground into the clouds. The warm air carries water vapor. 1

As the water vapor cools, it becomes liquid water. When the drops of water are big enough, rain begins to fall. 2

The drops of water in the clouds are charged with electricity. As the drops move in the clouds, their charge builds up and grows. Suddenly, there is a discharge of electricity that causes a flash of lightning! 3

The flash of lightning heats up the air around it. The hot air crashes into the cooler air around it. When the air moves, it creates sound waves. Then there is a loud crash of thunder! 4

A Few Words About Weather
(Building Vocabulary)

Your budding meteorologists are sure to become storm experts with this vocabulary-building activity! Provide a copy of page 30 for each student. Have her color and cut out the pieces. Next, direct the child to carefully cut along the dashed lines on the television screen. Instruct her to gently thread the definition strip through the top slots and the word strip through the bottom slots as shown. Then have her pull the strips to match each word, in turn, to its definition. Ask each student to read her words and definitions with a partner before she takes her television vocabulary screen home to share with her family!

Lightning Safety
(Understanding Lightning Safety)

Enlighten students about the precautions that they should take during thunderstorms with this safety poster. Make a list on chart paper or a transparency of the safety tips listed at the bottom of this page. Read and discuss each tip with the class. Provide a copy of page 32 for each child. Have her color and cut out the two pieces. Help the student carefully cut each flap on the top piece. Next, instruct the student to carefully stack the two pieces and line up their edges. Then have her glue the top piece over the bottom piece.

Give each child a 12" x 18" sheet of colorful construction paper. Have her glue her lightning safety scene to the top of the poster. Next, instruct the student to examine the pictures in the scene. Direct her to write each pictured tip on a sheet of writing paper and glue the writing paper to the bottom of the poster. Display the pictures on a bulletin board for an at-a-glance reminder of lightning safety!

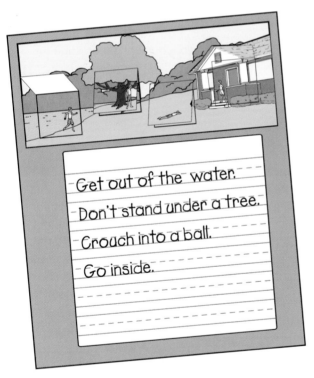

Get out of the water.
Don't stand under a tree.
Crouch into a ball.
Go inside.

Lightning Safety

- Do not talk on the telephone during a thunderstorm. *Lightning can travel through the telephone wires.*
- Seek shelter, preferably inside a large building.
- Stay in your car and roll up the windows.
- If you're outside, do not lie down on the ground. Crouch into a ball. *Lightning usually strikes the highest thing in the area.*
- Stay away from water.
- Stay away from metal objects.
- Do not stand under a tree or any other tall object.

In the Eye of the Storm
(Demonstration)

Which storm produces winds of 74 miles per hour or more, yet remains calm in the center? A hurricane. Follow the steps to demonstrate this storm phenomenon for students.

Materials needed:
large, clear, glass mixing bowl filled three-fourths
   full of water
black pepper
wooden spoon
ruler with a hole in the middle
6" length of string
paper clip
tape

Directions:
1. Tie one end of the string to the paper clip.
2. Thread the other end of the string through the hole in the middle of the ruler. Adjust the string until the paper clip is hanging on a length that is one inch shorter than the depth of the water in the bowl. Secure the string to the ruler with tape.
3. Sprinkle a generous amount of pepper in the water.
4. Stir the water until it is swirling.
5. Quickly lower the paper clip into the center of the bowl until the ruler rests on its edges. Lead the class in a discussion of the results. *(The water will continue to swirl around. However, the paper clip will move only gently, or not at all. Explain to students that, in the same way, the air inside the eye of a hurricane remains calm while winds swirl around it.)*

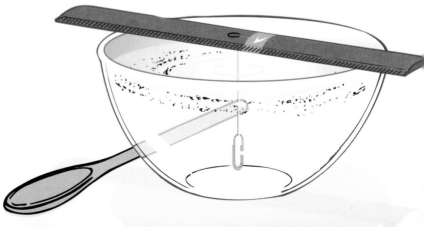

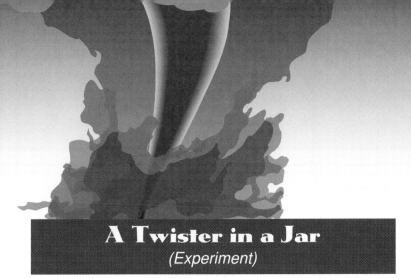

A Twister in a Jar
(Experiment)

These portable tornadoes provide students with hands-on learning about funnel clouds! Explain to students that the *vortex* of a tornado is created when different wind conditions at different altitudes make the updrafts in a thunderstorm spin. When the vortex dips below the bottom of the cloud, a funnel cloud is formed. When the funnel cloud touches the ground, it is called a tornado. To make individual tornadoes, guide each student through the steps shown.

Materials needed for each child:
1 clean, empty 16-oz. plastic bottle with lid
water
3 drops of food coloring
1 spoonful of dishwashing detergent
5 plastic beads

Directions:
1. Remove the label from the bottle.
2. Fill the bottle three-fourths full of water.
3. Add the detergent, the food coloring, and the beads.
4. Tightly screw the lid back on the bottle.
5. Twirl the bottle vigorously in a circular motion for about 15 seconds.
6. Quickly set the bottle upright on a flat surface. Presto! A mini funnel cloud!

During the Storm
(Literature, Sequencing, Recalling Events)

Come a Tide by George Ella Lyon (Orchard Books, 1993) is the entertaining story of a storm in a rural community. As you read the book aloud, discuss the events with students.

Provide a copy of page 33 for each child and invite different students to read each booklet page aloud. Instruct each child to cut out the booklet pages on the bold lines. Have him personalize the front page and then sequentially number and stack the booklet pages according to the order of events. Direct him to staple the pages on the side. Have the child draw and color a picture on each booklet page to match the sentence on that page.

Patterns

Use with "A Few Words About Weather" on page 27.

Television

Name _____

©2000 The Education Center, Inc. • *Investigating Science* • *Weather* • TEC1746

Word Strip	Definition Strip
Thunderstorm	Whirling funnel clouds that spin across land. Their wind speeds can reach up to 300 miles per hour.
Tornado	Falling or blowing snow with very cold temperatures and strong winds.
Hurricane	Violent rainstorms with thunder and lightning.
Blizzard	Huge spinning storms that can be hundreds of miles wide. These storms begin over tropical waters.

Word Strip

Definition Strip

©2000 The Education Center, Inc. • *Investigating Science* • *Weather* • TEC1746

Cloud

Information Cards

On hot, still days, warm air rises quickly from the ground into the clouds. The warm air carries water vapor. <div align="right">1</div>	As the water vapor cools, it becomes liquid water. When the drops of water are big enough, rain begins to fall. <div align="right">2</div>
The drops of water in the clouds are charged with electricity. As the drops move in the clouds, their charge builds up and grows. Suddenly, there is a discharge of electricity that causes a flash of lightning! <div align="right">3</div>	The flash of lightning heats up the air around it. The hot air crashes into the cooler air around it. When the air moves, it creates sound waves. Then there is a loud crash of thunder! <div align="right">4</div>

Patterns

Use with "Lightning Safety" on page 28.

Bottom Piece

Top Piece

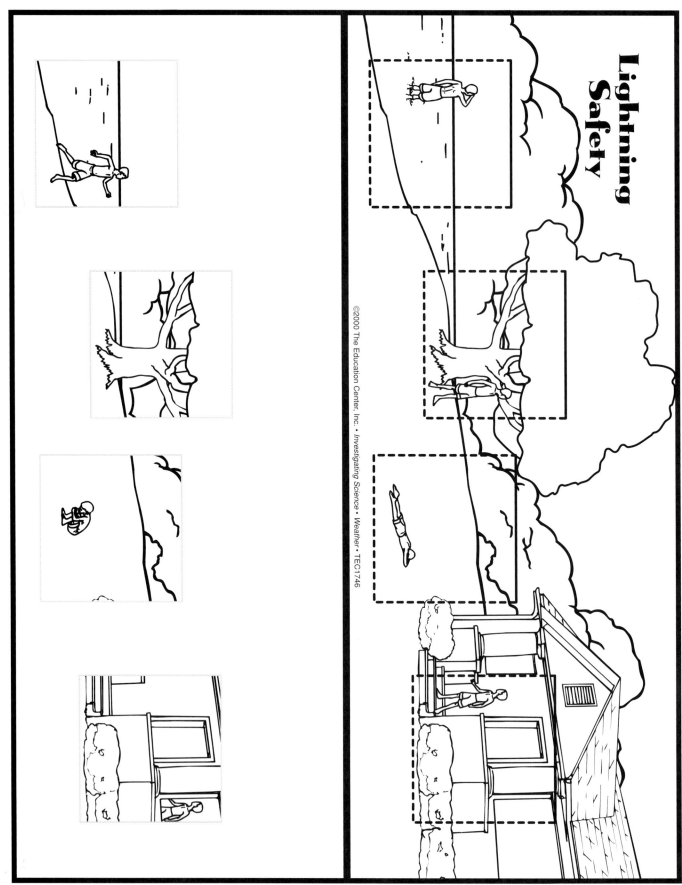

Lightning Safety

©2000 The Education Center, Inc. • *Investigating Science* • *Weather* • TEC1746

Come a Tide

Name _____

The family went to sleep with the radio on.

The people cleaned up the damage from the storm.

The warning whistle blew once!

It snowed and then it rained for four days.

The family spent the night at Grandma's house on the hill.

The Seasons

With this collection of activities and reproducibles, your students are sure to find out new and amazing facts about the seasons!

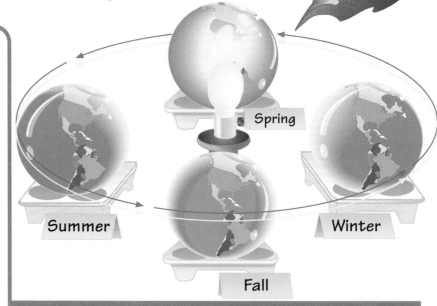

Background for the Teacher

- Seasons occur in four periods, or *climatic seasons,* based on temperature and weather changes throughout the year.
- Each of the seasons—spring, summer, autumn, and winter—lasts about three months and usually causes a change in the temperature, weather, and amount of daylight for most places on earth.
- The climatic seasons in the Southern Hemisphere and the Northern Hemisphere differ by about six months. The Southern Hemisphere has winter when the Northern Hemisphere has summer.
- Some regions on earth have temperatures that vary little, so they do not have all four seasons.
- Tropical regions experience wet and dry seasons based on the amount of rainfall.
- Polar regions experience light and dark seasons based on the amount of daylight.
- In the Northern Hemisphere each season officially begins as follows: summer—June 20 or 21 on the *summer solstice,* autumn—September 22 or 23 on the *autumnal equinox,* winter—December 21 or 22 on the *winter solstice,* and spring—March 20 or 21 on the *vernal equinox.*

Shining Seasons
(Demonstration)

Use this easy demonstration to shine some light on how the four seasons occur. To begin, explain to your students that the earth's *axis*—an imaginary line through the center of the earth that the earth rotates around—tilts as the earth *revolves* around the sun. Further explain that the earth takes 365 days, or one year, to make a revolution around the sun. Because it tilts as it revolves, different areas of the earth are closer to the sun and receive more of the sun's rays than other areas throughout a year. This difference is what causes the four seasons.

Show students how the earth's tilt and its revolutions around the sun determine each season by setting up the following demonstration. Purchase four inflatable globes from your local teacher's supply store. Also ask a fast-food restaurant to donate four four-cup cardboard beverage flats. Obtain a tall table lamp with at least a 75-watt lightbulb, and remove its shade. Plug in the lamp and place it in a large open area on the floor to represent the sun. Then set each inflatable globe on a beverage flat, tilting it toward the lamp as shown. Set a construction paper sign near each globe indicating the season. Next, have your students gather around the demonstration area; then dim the lights and turn on the lamp. Beginning with the globe labeled "Summer," point out to students how the sun's rays are shining directly on North America, causing hot weather and longer days. Continue to explain the sun's rays in relation to each season in the display. Finally, further extend this lesson by providing each student with a copy of page 38 to complete as directed.

Seasonal Selections

Autumn Across America (Seasons Across America series) by Seymour Simon (Hyperion Books for Children, 1993)
A Bear for All Seasons by Diane Marcial Fuchs (Henry Holt and Company, 1995)
Discover the Seasons by Diane Iverson (Dawn Publications, 1996)
Gather Up, Gather In: A Book of Seasons by M. C. Helldorfer (Puffin Books, 1998)
Ring of Earth: A Child's Book of Seasons by Jane Yolen (Harcourt Brace Jovanovich, Publishers; 1986)
The Seasons and Someone by Virginia Kroll (Harcourt Brace & Company, 1994)

Creative Calendars
(Working With Calendar Days)

Use this activity to help your youngsters become more familiar with calendar days and the important events within each season. Ahead of time program the name of each month and season on a separate sentence strip. Display the strips where every student can view them. Then with students' help, arrange the months into groups based on the seasons they generally fall under.

Next, provide each child with a computer-generated calendar for each month of the year. Encourage the student to group her calendars into seasonal sets. Next, give each child four sheets of construction paper. Help the student staple a sheet on top of each set of calendars. Direct the student to title each cover with the season name and then use markers or crayons to decorate it with a seasonal picture. Choose two or three holidays or events in each season. Help each student locate the correct dates in her seasonal booklet and write the name of each event. Collect the booklets and store them by season. Then at the beginning of each season, give each student her seasonal booklet and encourage her to keep track of the days and the important events.

Global Opposites
(Understanding Hemispheres)

Help your students understand how the earth's Northern and Southern Hemispheres experience opposite seasons with this hands-on activity. Begin by using a globe to point out the Northern and Southern Hemispheres to students. Discuss with them how the people in the Southern Hemisphere and the people in the Northern Hemisphere have opposite seasons during the same time. Next, provide each student with two enlarged copies of the earth pattern and the materials listed. Guide students through the directions to create opposite-season mobiles.

Materials for each student: 2 large blue construction paper circle cutouts (each slightly larger than the enlarged earth pattern), 1 sheet of tissue paper, 3 lengths of yarn, 2 blank index cards, hole puncher, glue, scissors, stapler, markers or crayons

Directions:
1. Glue each earth pattern onto a blue construction paper cutout.
2. At the top of one pattern, write "Summer." Write "Winter" at the bottom.
3. At the top of the other pattern, write "Winter." Write "Summer" at the bottom.
4. On the lines write a sentence describing the season in each hemisphere. Color each hemisphere.
5. On one index card write "Summer in the Northern Hemisphere" on one side and "Winter in the Southern Hemisphere" on the other side. On the other card write "Winter in the Northern Hemisphere" on one side and "Summer in the Southern Hemisphere" on the other. Add a picture showing activities people might do in each hemisphere during each season. Punch one hole in the top of each card.
6. Staple the two circles together back-to-back, leaving an opening near the top. Stuff the circles with tissue paper and staple them closed. Punch one hole at the top of the earth shape and two at the bottom.
7. Thread one end of a yarn piece through the hole at the top of the earth shape and tie a small knot. Thread one end of a yarn piece through the hole in each index card and tie a small knot. Thread the other end through a hole at the bottom of the earth shape, and tie a small knot to secure each index card to the earth shape.

Help students grasp the difference between seasons and daily weather with this table- and graph-making activity. Begin by sharing the background information (page 34) with students. Further explain that even though certain types of weather generally occur during specific seasons (snow during winter), some kinds of weather can occur in every season. Ahead of time make and copy an observation table similar to the one shown for each student. Then have students observe daily weather patterns. Have the student write a prediction about which types of weather he thinks will occur and how often in one week during the current season. Then direct the student to record daily weather on his table for seven days. At the end of the week, use the information from the students' tables to create a class graph like the one shown. Discuss with students which types of weather were most common. If desired, provide each student with a table for a week during each season. Direct the child to record his predictions and daily weather observations for that week. Then create class graphs showing the most common weather for that season. Finally, compare the four seasonal graphs and ask students to determine the most common weather occurrences throughout the year.

Prediction 7 snowy days	Winter Weather
Monday	
Tuesday	Sunny, cold
Wednesday	Cloudy, cold
Thursday	Cloudy, cold
Friday	Snow
Saturday	Cloudy, cool
Sunday	Sunny, cool
	Snow

Sean Smith

Winter Weather Week (Dec. 1–8)

	sunny	hot	rainy	warm	cold	cool	cloudy	windy	snowy
Monday	X				X				
Tuesday					X		X		
Wednesday					X		X		
Thursday									X
Friday						X	X		
Saturday	X						X		
Sunday									X

Materials for each group: one 14" x 8" sheet of white paper, one 12" x 18" sheet of construction paper, ruler, glue, scissors, markers or crayons

Directions:

1. Fold the sheet of white paper in half vertically, leaving one side a half inch shorter than the other side.
2. Measure and mark four 3½-inch sections along the paper as shown. Cut apart the sections and give one to each group member.
3. Fold the tab up similar to a matchbook. Write information about your topic on the inside of your section. Add the title and a picture about your topic on the front flap.
4. Glue each section onto the sheet of construction paper. Title the sheet with the name of your group's season and decorate it.

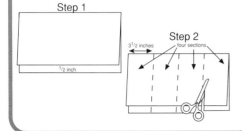

Step 1

Step 2

3½ inches   four sections

½ inch

Can't Stop Change
(Writing)

Help your students explore how people, animals, places, and activities are affected by changes in the seasons. To begin, divide students into groups of four and assign each group a season. Direct the group to write each of the following headings at the top of a sheet of paper: *Weather, Clothing, Plants and Animals,* and *Activities.* Instruct each group member to choose a category sheet and then list information on his sheet about how the season affects that category. Next, have the groups make fact-filled charts like the one shown. Provide the groups with the materials listed and guide them through the directions. Set aside time for each group to share its chart with the class. Discuss how the information in each category changed depending on the season. As a fun follow-up activity, pair students and provide each pair with a copy of the game on pages 40 and 41.

Summer

Weather   Clothing

Plants & Animals

swimming

playing baseball

Step 4

Picture-Perfect Seasons
(Reading, Writing)

Help your students picture the seasons in a more personal way with this activity. First, obtain a copy of the book *When Summer Comes* by Robert Maass (Henry Holt and Company, Inc.; 1996) or another seasonal title in the same series. Read the book to your students and discuss the photographs. Then ask each student to bring to class a picture of herself taken during the summer. Have each child use double-sided tape to attach her photograph to a sheet of white construction paper. Direct the student to write one or two sentences below her picture describing what's best about summer, similar to the text and descriptions in the book. Display the pictures and sentences on a bulletin board titled "When Summer Comes..."

When Summer Con

I like to build sand castles at the beach.

I like to swim in the lake with my brother.

Recipes for All Seasons
(Cooking)

Here are four tasty, easy-to-make treats that can be enjoyed by your students on the first day of each season! Explain to students that in the Northern Hemisphere, the first day of summer (June 20 or 21) is called the *summer solstice,* the first day of autumn (September 22 or 23) is known as the *autumnal equinox,* the first day of winter (December 21 or 22) is called the *winter solstice,* and the first day of spring (March 20 or 21) is the *vernal equinox.* (Check a current calendar to find out the date of the beginning of each season.) On each date allow students to make and eat the seasonal snack below.

Spring Chicks

Ingredients:
1 corn muffin per child
honey butter
2 M&M's® brand mini baking bits per child
3 pieces of candy corn per child

Student Directions:
1. Spread the honey butter onto the corn muffin.
2. Place the M&M's onto the muffin to make eyes.
3. Put one candy corn piece on the muffin as a beak. Push the other candy corn pieces into the corn muffin as feet.
4. Enjoy!

Summer Sunshine Salad

Ingredients:
2–3 spoonfuls pineapple tidbits per child
2–3 spoonfuls banana slices per child
2–3 spoonfuls lemon yogurt per child
shredded coconut (tinted yellow with food coloring)
1/4 c. orange juice per child (measured into a Styrofoam® bowl)

Student Directions:
1. Spoon the yogurt into the bowl; then mix with the juice.
2. Spoon the pineapple and banana slices into the bowl. Mix together.
3. Sprinkle a pinch of coconut into the bowl and mix.
4. Enjoy!

Autumn Apple Toast

Ingredients:
a tub of butter
1 apple quarter for every child (sliced ahead of time into four pieces)
1 whole-wheat bread slice per child
cinnamon-sugar mixture in a shaker

Student Directions:
1. Spread butter on the bread.
2. Place the apple slices on top of the bread.
3. Shake the cinnamon-sugar mixture onto the apples.
4. Place the bread on a cookie sheet for your teacher to toast.
5. Enjoy!

White Winter Snack

Ingredients:
soft cream cheese
1 chocolate wafer per child
flaked coconut
prepared hot chocolate (one cup per child)

Student Directions:
1. Spread the cream cheese on the wafer.
2. Sprinkle the coconut onto the cream cheese.
3. Enjoy with a warm cup of hot chocolate.

The Fun Four

Directions:
Read each question below.
Write your answer on the
blank line. Then follow the
color code under each
question to color the four
seasonal pictures.

1. In what season does it snow the most? _____
   (Color *A* orange and *B* black.)

2. In what season do we celebrate the Fourth of July? _____
   (Color *C* blue and *D* red.)

3. In what season is the month of May? _____
   (Color *E* pink and *F* green.)

4. In what season do leaves change colors? _____
   (Color *G* orange and *H* brown.)

5. In what season do some animals hibernate? _____
   (Color *I* blue and *J* purple.)

6. In what season is the temperature the hottest? _____
   (Color *K* yellow and *L* green.)

7. In what season are many baby animals born? _____
   (Color *M* brown and *N* green.)

8. In what season do leaves fall from trees? _____
   (Color *O* yellow and *P* red.)

©2000 The Education Center, Inc. • *Investigating Science* • *Weather* • TEC1746 • Key p. 48

38   **Note to the teacher:** Use with "Shining Seasons" on page 34.

Get Clear on the Hemispheres

The earth is divided by the equator into the *Northern* and *Southern Hemispheres*. These hemispheres have opposite seasons. Color the map key. Then color the map. Use the map to answer the questions.

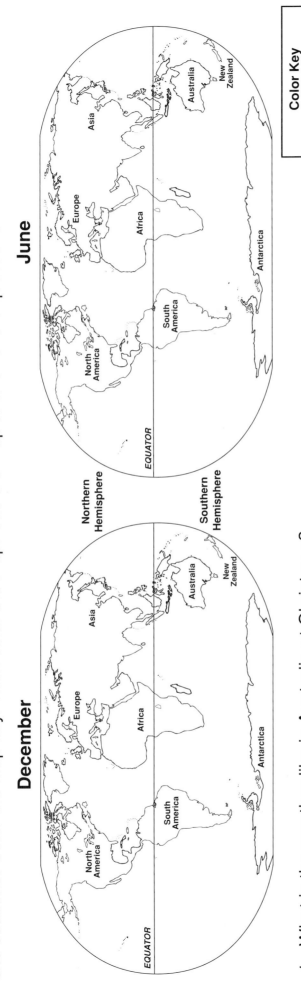

December

June

Color Key

yellow	equator
blue	oceans
red	Northern Hemisphere winter
green	Southern Hemisphere summer
green	Northern Hemisphere summer
red	Southern Hemisphere winter

1. What is the weather like in Australia at Christmas? _____

2. List three places on the map that have summer in December. _____

3. What seasons does South America have in June? _____

4. List three places on the map that have summer in June. _____

5. Would you like to have winter weather in June and summer weather in December where you live? Why or why not? _____

Seasonal Squares

Directions for two players:
1. Put your game pieces on START.
2. Take turns rolling the die.
3. Read and follow the directions in the space you land on.
4. When both players reach the Welcome sign, the game is over.

It's an ice storm! Go back two spaces.	
It's too cold to go outside. Pretend you are shivering.	
The leaves are back. It's spring. Hop in place two times.	

Tell your partner three activities you do in the winter.

Winter is here. Clap your hands if you like snow.

S
T
A
R
T

Thunder-storms scare you. Go back to START.

You spot a bird's eggs. Go ahead two spaces.

Welcome to a new year!

You pick spring flow-ers. Smile at your partner.

Winter is almost here. Go forward one space.

It's a record 98°F today—too hot to play! Go back four spaces.

Hooray! It's the Fourth of July. Pretend you are wav-ing a flag.

It's a windy autumn day. Cover your eyes with your hands.

Back to school! Laugh as if you are happy.

You have a sunburn. Go back three spaces.

The ice-cream truck is here. Go forward two spaces.

The leaves start falling from trees. Go back three spaces.

©2000 The Education Center, Inc. • *Investigating Science • Weather* • TEC1746

Note to the teacher: Use with "Can't Stop Change" on page 36. Duplicate this page for each pair and provide the pair with two game pieces. Use with the cube on page 41.

Directions:

1. Color the pictures on the cube.
2. Carefully cut out the cube pattern along the bold lines.
3. Place the pattern printed side up on your desk. Fold along the dotted lines to form a cube. (The pictures should be on the outside of the cube.)
4. Glue the tabs to the inside of the cube.

Roll again.

Lose a turn.

TAB

TAB

TAB

TAB

TAB

TAB

Note to the teacher: Use with "Seasonal Squares" on page 40. Remind students that the Sun = 1, leaves = 2, etc.

Weather Forecasting

Encourage your students to become meteorologically minded as they practice predicting the weather with these activities and experiments.

Background for the Teacher

- Weather is the condition of the *atmosphere*—the invisible blanket of air that surrounds the earth.
- *Meteorologists* are scientists who use instruments—such as radar, satellites, and computers—to study and then forecast the weather.
- The National Weather Service in the United States and the Atmospheric Environment Service in Canada issue weather forecasts.
- Observation stations around the world use different instruments to record weather conditions. *Thermometers* measure air temperature, *barometers* show air pressure, *weather vanes* show wind direction, *anemometers* measure wind speed, *hygrometers* measure air moisture, and *rain gauges* measure rainfall or snowfall.
- Weather forecasts help people plan their daily activities and enable many people to do their jobs more efficiently.
- Weather forecasts save many lives with warnings and watches for extreme conditions.
- Weather maps appear in many U.S. daily newspapers, on television broadcasts, and on the Internet to show expected short-range and extended weather conditions for the nation.
- Weather conditions depend on four elements: temperature, air pressure, wind, and moisture.

Meteorologist Mixer
(Observation, Weather Chart)

Introduce your students to weather watching as they practice scientific process skills. In advance, make a copy of "Weather Watchin' Station" on page 46 for each child. Explain that a *meteorologist* is a scientist who collects information about the atmosphere using different scientific instruments. Further explain that meteorologists observe weather conditions to make accurate forecasts. Have each child practice observing and collecting weather data by recording weather conditions on his weather chart for five days. Help students complete the chart using the activities and experiments in this unit. Then invite your junior meteorologists to analyze their data with "Mapping It" on page 45.

Literary Forecast

How's the Weather? A Look at Weather and How It Changes by Melvin and Gilda Berger (Ideals Children's Books, 1993)

Weather and Climate by Barbara Taylor (Kingfisher Books, 1993)

Weather Forecasting by Gail Gibbons (Aladdin Paperbacks, 1993)

Weather Words and What They Mean by Gail Gibbons (Scholastic Inc., 1990)

What Will the Weather Be? by Lynda DeWitt (HarperTrophy, 1991)

Temperature Tools
(Experiment, Collecting Data)

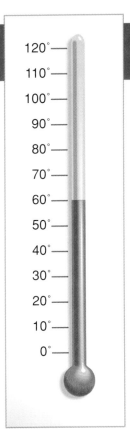

Jump into your study of weather with this estimation and observation activity. You'll need a thermometer and a cricket. Intrigue your students with the idea that a cricket could be referred to as nature's thermometer because the rate at which it chirps changes when the temperature changes. Explain that the Fahrenheit temperature can be estimated by adding 40 to the number of times a cricket chirps in 14 seconds. After counting the number of times the cricket chirps and adding 40 to the number, ask students to check the temperature estimate with an actual thermometer.

For more practice observing temperature changes, place the thermometer outside. Instruct a small group of students to read and report the temperature three times a day. Have all students record the data on their weather charts, and then mark the lowest temperature with an "L" and the highest temperature with an "H."

Under Pressure
(Making a Barometer, Recording Data)

Help your students *see* the effect that temperature has on air pressure with this experiment. Explain that air pressure is the force of the air pressing down on the earth, and changes in it cause changes in the weather. Have a small group of students follow the steps below to make a *barometer* —an instrument that measures the pressure of the atmosphere.

Materials:
wide-mouthed plastic jar
balloon
rubber band
drinking straw
2" x 8" strip of poster board
marker
tape
ruler
scissors

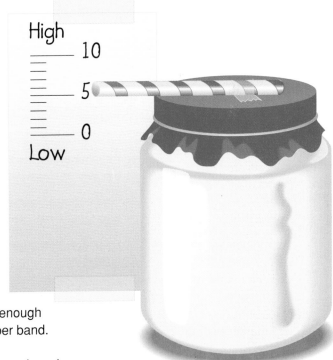

Steps:
1. Inflate and deflate the balloon, and then cut a piece large enough to stretch over the top of the container. Secure with a rubber band.
2. Tape the straw to the middle of the balloon as shown.
3. Use a ruler and marker to draw the scale shown on the poster board.
4. Place the barometer and scale side by side, taping the scale in place.
5. Check the barometer at the same time daily. Have students record on their weather charts if the air pressure is up, down, or steady.

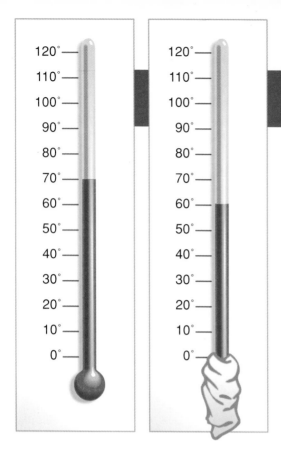

Humidly Speaking
(Humidity Experiment)

It's all relative when you're talking about humidity! Try this experiment to demonstrate how humidity affects air temperature. Explain to students that *humidity* refers to the water vapor in the air; the more moisture in the air, the higher the humidity.

To prepare, collect two thermometers, a wet cloth, and a piece of poster board. Place the thermometers side by side, undisturbed for five minutes, and record the temperatures. Then wrap the wet cloth around the bulb of one thermometer. Use the poster board to fan both thermometers for two minutes; observe and then record the temperatures. The thermometer with the wet cloth will have a lower temperature because the water in the cloth is evaporating into the air surrounding it.

Hair-Raising Hygrometer
(Making a Hygrometer)

Did you know your hair is a weather indicator? Ask a student to donate a strand of hair to complete this hair hygrometer experiment. Explain that meteorologists use a *hygrometer* to measure humidity in the air. Hair is a good indicator because it absorbs moisture from the air and stretches as the humidity increases.

Materials:
large glass jar without lid
straight strand of hair (4"–5" long)
flat toothpick
tape
markers
pencil

Steps:
1. Color the pointed end of the toothpick with a marker.
2. Tape one end of the hair to the middle of the toothpick and tape the other end to the middle of the pencil.
3. Place the pencil on top of the jar with the toothpick hanging down horizontally inside it.
4. Use a marker to draw a line on the outside of the jar to mark the level of the toothpick.
5. Observe the toothpick daily for the next five days. Use a different-colored marker each day to draw a line on the jar to record the humidity level.
6. Have students record the humidity level on their weather charts.

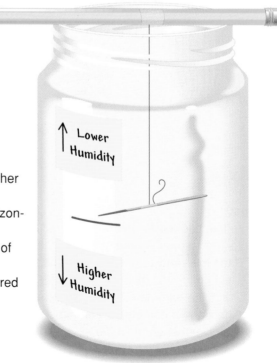

Windy Way
(Making an Anemometer)

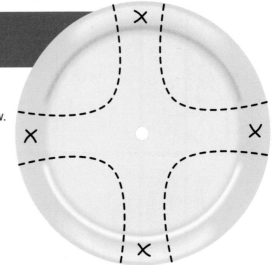

Capturing the wind and measuring its strength is a breeze with this experiment. Explain that a meteorologist uses an *anemometer* to measure wind speed. Create a simple anemometer by following the directions below.

Materials:

ballpoint-pen cap	scissors
large Styrofoam® plate	pencil
four 3-oz. paper cups	stopwatch
(paint one cup a different color)	stapler

Steps:

1. Cut out four U-shaped sections from the plate and mark the plate with Xs as shown.
2. Staple one cup onto each X, making sure they all face the same direction.
3. Use scissors to make a hole in the center of the plate large enough to push the pen cap through securely.
4. Put the pen cap and cutout plate on top of the pencil, and then spin the cutout to ensure it rotates easily.
5. To determine if the wind is fast, slow, or calm, take the anemometer outside and count the number of times the colored cup passes the same spot in ten seconds. The higher the number, the stronger the wind.
6. Have students record their observations on their weather charts.

Mapping It
(Creating a Weather Map)

Your students will pull all their weather know-how together with this weather map activity. In advance, obtain five copies of a newspaper weather map, make five four-inch tagboard tracers of your state, and copy the weather map on page 47 for each child. Explain that a meteorologist analyzes information collected from different weather instruments to make the weather maps seen on television and in the newspaper.

Give each child a copy of page 47. Next, divide students into five groups, and give each group one state tracer and one newspaper weather map. Instruct each student to trace the state in the space on page 47. Ask each group to study the newspaper weather map and then re-create it on the U.S. map, using the correct weather symbols. Finally, assign each group a different day from the "Weather Watchin' Station" chart. Have the group create state weather maps for its assigned day, using the weather information gathered and the weather symbols key.

Wonderful Weather Web Sites

CNN Weather Forecasts
http://www.cnn.com./weather

The Weather Channel
http://www.weather.com/education

National Weather Service
http://www.nws.noaa.gov/

USA Today Weather
http://www.usatoday.com/weather

Name _____

Weather Watchin' Station

Day	Conditions	Temperature	Barometer (air pressure)	Hygrometer (humidity)	Anemometer (wind speed)	My forecast for tomorrow
		1. _____ 2. _____ 3. _____	☐ Up ☐ Steady ☐ Down	☐ Higher ☐ Steady ☐ Lower	☐ Slow ☐ Calm ☐ Fast	
		1. _____ 2. _____ 3. _____	☐ Up ☐ Steady ☐ Down	☐ Higher ☐ Steady ☐ Lower	☐ Slow ☐ Calm ☐ Fast	
		1. _____ 2. _____ 3. _____	☐ Up ☐ Steady ☐ Down	☐ Higher ☐ Steady ☐ Lower	☐ Slow ☐ Calm ☐ Fast	
		1. _____ 2. _____ 3. _____	☐ Up ☐ Steady ☐ Down	☐ Higher ☐ Steady ☐ Lower	☐ Slow ☐ Calm ☐ Fast	
		1. _____ 2. _____ 3. _____	☐ Up ☐ Steady ☐ Down	☐ Higher ☐ Steady ☐ Lower	☐ Slow ☐ Calm ☐ Fast	

Weather Conditions

sunny   partly cloudy   cloudy   rain   snow   thunderstorm

©2000 The Education Center, Inc. • Investigating Science • Weather • TEC1746

Note to the teacher: Have students use this chart to record data they collect from the weather experiments and activities on pages 42–45.

Name _____

United States Weather Map

My State Weather Map

for _____
(date)

(Trace your state shape here.)

not to scale

Weather Symbols Key

| 49/32 | high and low temperature |
| rain |
| thunderstorm |
| snow |
| sunny |

cloudy

partly cloudy

H high pressure

L low pressure

windy

Note to the teacher: Use with "Mapping It" on page 45.

Answer Keys

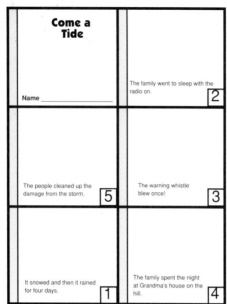

Come a Tide	The family went to sleep with the radio on.
Name _____	2
The people cleaned up the damage from the storm.	The warning whistle blew once!
5	3
It snowed and then it rained for four days.	The family spent the night at Grandma's house on the hill.
1	4

Page 38

1. winter
2. summer
3. spring
4. fall
5. winter
6. summer
7. spring
8. fall

Page 39

1. warm
2. southern South America, southern Africa, Australia, New Zealand, Antarctica
3. fall and winter
4. North America, northern Africa, Europe, Asia, northern South America
5. Students' answers will vary.

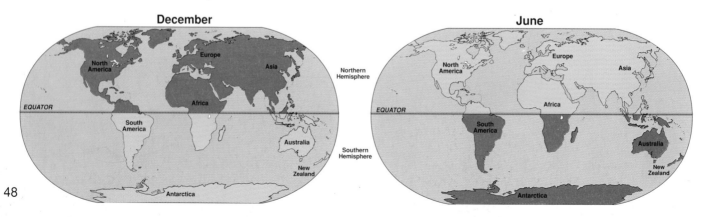